# How to Succeed in Voice-Overs Without Ever Losing

By:

Jack Angel

abbott press®
A DIVISION OF WRITER'S DIGEST

**How to Succeed in Voice-Overs**
**Without Ever Losing**

*ISBN: 978-1-4582-0321-2 (sc)*
*ISBN: 978-1-4582-0320-5 (e)*

*Library of Congress Control Number: 2012906423*

*Abbott Press books may be ordered through booksellers or by contacting:*

*Abbott Press*
*1663 Liberty Drive*
*Bloomington, IN 47403*
*www.abbottpress.com*
*Phone: 1-866-697-5310*

*Printed in the United States of America*

*Abbott Press rev. date:4/30/2012*

# Contents

# FOREWORD

The purpose of this book is to inspire its readers and to put them in charge of their careers, as well as to create a context for winning, no matter what happens. If you were writing such a book, you would not put anything into it that wasn't intended to further that purpose. In this book, there may be times you sense that we've gone astray, but I assure you, if you stick with me, it will all come together

My experience has been in the voice-over end of acting in Hollywood. So that's the basis for most of the material in the book. Voice is a microcosm of the whole acting process. There's the audition, the callback, the job itself, and the payoffs—except that it all happens in a matter of a couple of days, and there are no costumes or makeup to contend with and no memorization. So everything in this book is applicable to any facet of acting and, in fact, any other profession. Just change the labels.

Then there is the question of who in the hell am I to presume to write such a book? Well, I've been doing "voice" work for over fifty years. And over that period of time I've worked with Lucas Arts, Disney, Pixar, Warner Brothers, Marvel, Steven Speilberg and many more. I also enjoyed ten years as an NBC promo announcer and eighteen years as a major West Coast disc jockey.. At the end of this book there's a copy of my résumé. Every time I look at it, even *I'm* impressed. (Also, if you go online to www.jackangel.com and click on resources, then the "by the numbers" link, you will see that of all the actors who appeared in movies that grossed over $100 million, at this writing I'm ranked number six. If that doesn't impress you, nothing will.)

I suppose if you were writing a book on a particular subject, it might be helpful to define what it is you're going to talk about. When I first heard the term "voice-over," it referred to that disembodied voice on television commercials—the voice, over the picture. But in the years since, it has come to mean everything voice artists do, including TV commercials and promos, radio, animation, and narrations.

# OH, BUT IT'S SO HARD TO BREAK IN

I can't tell you how many times I've heard people say, "You can't break into voice-overs. It's a closed profession." Well, it may look that way, but guess what? All you have to say is, "I'm in!" and everyone will scooch over a tad to make room for you.

Of course, we'll eat you alive if you jump in without knowing what you're doing. That's why classes were invented. So take a few classes, learn the language of the game, and become familiar with the microphones and headsets and copy stands and all the other equipment with which you'll come in contact. And bear in mind that your teacher is only right some of the time. Nothing is carved in stone.

Then, practice, practice, practice! When I was new to radio, I used to read billboards aloud on my way to work. That served to get me warmed up and kept me sharp.

Another objection that people sometimes raise sounds like this: "But I don't have the kind of voice they're looking for." Well, listen to the voices on TV. Listen to the voices on *The Simpsons*. They're all different, and they're all weird.

At one time in the business, Marty Ingels had what I felt was the worst announcer's voice I'd ever heard. I thought he sounded like he'd gargled with razor blades. Orson Welles, on the other hand, with those mellifluous tones, had the best, and everybody else fell somewhere in-between. On then-current commercials, Welles delivered with such authority, "The Wings of Man," the slogan for Eastern Airlines. Marty, with his gravelly voice, did a pitch for house paint. I thought that if you transposed them, the spots would have been different, but they would have worked. Hearing Marty saying, "The Wings of Man," and seeing Orson Welles on a ladder with a paint brush in his hand would have been priceless.

Truly, anything goes.

Go to www.arlenethornton.com and listen to some of the voice people Arlene represents. I suggest Arlene Thornton's Web site for a couple of reasons. First, because Arlene is my agent, and I'm on the site. (I know the other voice artists on the website, too. I know how good they are, and I know you can learn from just hearing them perform.) Second, as of this writing—and as amazing as it may seem—no other top agency in Hollywood has such a complete and interactive voice-over web presence.

For people just getting started, one of the most intimidating things is to stand on the soundstage all by yourself, watching four or five people in the recording booth discussing whatever after your first take. You can't hear them, so you don't know what they're saying, but they're quite animated, and in your insecurity you're positive they're saying, "Where the hell did you get this guy? Couldn't we get Jack Angel? What'll we do now? Well, have him do a couple of more takes and we'll get rid of him."

They are never saying that, but out of your insecurity your imagination will make up all kinds of horror stories. So, when you're new to the game and you're in that situation, make up this conversation: "Oh, my God! He's fabulous! We'll have to give him all our accounts." Or, "Let's sign her to a seven-year contract now, before her price goes up."

They are never saying that, either. But isn't that better than the alternative? This way, you're ready when the director says, "Take two."

This brings me to another point.

After an audition, some casting directors will tell you that your reading was "fabulous." They'll go on and on about how you were right on! Terrific! Wonderful! Actors then go back to their agents and say they think they booked the job, because the casting person was so complimentary about their audition. One casting director in particular has been doing this for years and says the same thing to almost everybody. Take compliments with a small grain of salt. You haven't booked the job until your agent says so.

# THERE AIN'T NO DAMN REJECTION

"There Ain't No Damn Rejection" was almost the title of this book, so I should devote some time to the idea. If you speak to most actors who are struggling to "make it" in Hollywood, you will most likely be told that the rejection is awful. In magazine articles and on interview shows, some very successful actors say the same thing.

The plain truth of the matter is that *there ain't no damn rejection!* The process of auditioning is one of *selection*, not rejection. *Rejection* happens only when you cause it.

If you show up drunk or ill-prepared, if you become unruly or surly, you will most certainly be rejected. But apart from that kind of unprofessional behavior on your part, think of auditioning as a process of selection—not impending rejection.

For example, if you and I are given the task of casting the role of Santa Claus, we will notify various agents to submit actors who physically meet our specifications; they should be roly-poly, jolly looking, elfin, and have a full voice for his "ho-ho-ho." And although we can attach a beard to anyone, it would help if the actor has already cultivated one—which should be white.

Now, a whole bunch of fat actors will show up. Some will be wearing Santa suits, but most won't. Some will have beards, and some won't. We'll look at all of them, talk to them, have them read the lines (if there are any), and then we'll select only one—the one you and I agree upon as the most Santa-like of the lot. We can select only one. All of the actors who weren't selected may go out into the world and say they were rejected. Who rejected them? Not us! We were in a process of selection. If they said they were rejected, they made it up.

Some will say, "I lost a good one today." But when did you ever lose something that was never yours in the first place? The role was theirs to win, and they didn't win it. What they did win, however, was the chance to be seen by a casting director who might very well choose them for another part in another project.

More than that, on the day the call went out, we wanted the best actors from each agency to show up. We never asked for anything less than the top guys in the business.

Nobody said, "Send me a bunch of so-so actors." So, if twenty Santas showed up, all were the best in the business. And in Los Angeles, New York, and Chicago (and from time to time, a few other cities around the country when they're producing national commercials), we're all playing at the level of "world class" .

Each time you're selected to audition, you are one of the best in the world. That's not rejection! In fact, it's great validation.

It's like this: when you enter the marketplace and you are the commodity, you're there to be bought (at least your talent is) if a buyer has a notion to do so. You should look at it like that. If someone was going to the store to shop for breakfast food and chose Wheaties over Cheerios, they'd just be *selecting* the Wheaties. Of all the choices available on the shelves, the Wheaties suited them best *this time*. They may come back the next day and buy the Cheerios, or not. Buying Froot Loops doesn't mean they're rejecting the Cheerios, either. They're just *selecting*, not rejecting.

If you can tap into that idea, your auditions will be angst-free.

United States Senator Hubert Humphrey provides the ultimate rejection story to illustrate my point, even though his story has little to do with acting. After being elected and re-elected to the United States Senate year after year for decades, Hubert Humphrey became vice president of the United States and then ran for president. He lost the presidential election by something like two percent of the vote. In a career that spanned all those years, he eventually had lost for the first time. He then lamented to a newsperson that it was agonizing to offer oneself to the American people and be rejected by them. Almost one hundred million people chose him for the highest office in the land, but Humphrey called it rejection. Just like the actors who don't get selected for a role, Humphrey made it up.

# It Only Takes One Person

A good friend of mine, the late Danny Dark, was the voice of NBC for fifteen years. It only had taken one person (John Miller, the head of promotions at NBC) to decide that he didn't want to hear Danny on any other network. John put Danny under contract at NBC, and Danny made close to a million dollars a year while he was there. Danny was one of the best voice-over artists who ever lived, so he also made a bundle of money doing commercials and movie trailers, and he was the voice of Superman in the Hanna/Barbera cartoon series, *Superfriends*.

Here's a story that'll tug at your heartstrings—or purse strings. Danny and I both auditioned for the Budweiser beer account a few years ago. Danny won. The creative director at the time was Rich Levy, who by chance is the best friend of my wife's brother. Rich came to Los Angeles, and Arlene and I took him to dinner at a posh bistro—The Ivy in Beverly Hills.

During the course of the dinner, Rich said, "Oh, by the way, do you want to know how close you came to winning the Budweiser account?"

"Sure," I said. Rich moved his coffee cup about a quarter of an inch. He went on to say that there were six people in the selection process. Five wanted me, and one wanted

Danny. The head of the agency was the one who wanted Danny. Danny won. Then Rich asked if I wanted to know how much money I didn't make.

Arlene said, "No."

I said, "Yes."

"Well," Rich went on, "Darren McGavin had the account for a few years prior to this, and he had an annual guarantee of a million dollars, and each year he exceeded the guarantee."

That's the kind of account that will change your life.

Although Danny was "The Voice" of NBC, they did use other announcers in the promo department. As I mentioned earlier, I also worked at NBC for ten years. Do you want to know how easy it was to get that job?

I had auditioned and won the job as the show announcer for Michael Mann's *Crime Story* series. During the few weeks prior to the premiere, I was called upon to do a lot of pre-launch promos for the show. During that time NBC producers would ask me to voice other promos as well. Shortly thereafter NBC decided they needed a promo announcer for *The Tonight Show Starring Johnny Carson*. John Luma, the head of hiring promo announcers, called Arlene Thornton and asked for a list of names of qualified promo announcers. When she got to my name, John said, "Oh, we know Jack. He'll be fine."

So it was that easy to get that job. Just doing the *Tonight Show* promos alone netted me well over $100 thousand dollars a year.

After Jay Leno took over *The Tonight Show,* and they changed promo announcers, Paula Cwikly, who was in charge of daytime promos wanted me as the voice of the soap opera promos. Paula became my champion at NBC.

Once Paula left, the new guy in charge of hiring announcers said one day, "Jack's done it enough. Let's get someone else."

And as easy as it came to me, it ended. Everything has a beginning and an end, and so it was with my tenure at NBC. And adding ten years at NBC to my résumé didn't hurt my reputation one bit.

The late Charlie O'Donnell, the announcer on *Wheel of Fortune* ("You've just won thirty *thooousand* dollars") had been the show announcer for twenty-five years. He told me that when he got the offer for that show, he was at the end a long run on another show and had decided to visit family and friends in New Jersey. He had checked in at a hotel and nobody on the West Coast knew where he was. But somehow his agent found him, called, and asked him if he'd like the job.

It only takes one person, and you don't know which person that is, so you have to "create yourself" to all of them. That is, there are people in high places all over the country who might love what you do, but they don't even know you exist.

# CREDITS AND THE MAGIC WORD

Nobody hires "good." If people were looking for good actors, all the good actors you know would be working and the rest would be selling shoes. So how come bad actors are working and good actors are selling Nine Wests?

Obviously, something else is going on.

I think the credits game started when some poor schlump hired an actor for a part, and his boss called him on the carpet because of it.

"I hired him because he's good."

"Naw! We don't want good, we want *terrific*!"

How do you arrive at terrific? Obviously there has to be some method of measurement. If Disney hired him, he must be terrific. If Ford hired him, he must be terrific.

A couple of years after I started devoting all my time to voice-over, I had a week in which I worked several times every day. Since then I've had a lot of weeks like that, but this was the first. Add in auditions every day at my agent's office and at various casting offices and ad agencies, and it was a rather hectic week. When it was all over, I had the sense that I did and said the exact same things over and over again. Everything seemed the same. Except every job and every audition was different.

Then I got it. All the talk before, during, and after the session was the same. Only the content of the jobs itself was different. The introductions and salutations were always the same (We have one spot, two spots, whatever). In the booth were directors, producers, writers, sometimes even the client, along with the recording engineer.

"Take one."

"Okay, hold it."

Discussion in the booth.

"Hey, that was great, but it was too long. Do it again, and pick up three seconds. And you sounded rushed, so slow down your delivery."

"Okay, that was good, except you flubbed a word."

"Take three."

"Take four."

"That was great, but again you were long."

"Fantastic, but emphasize this word or that."

For every person in the booth, you will wind up doing at least one extra take, because at some point, everyone will offer his or her input. When you finally get to that moment where everything is terrific, with no buts, the game is over and everyone moves on. So "terrific" is the magic word. Terrific or any synonym.

Sometimes the director will just say, "Go home!" or "That's a wrap." But it means, "Terrific. We got it."

So if "terrific" is the magic word, develop a reputation of being terrific and you'll get more work.

Sometimes the car you drive or the clothing you wear helps to make you terrific.

*"Gee, if she drives an MBZ SL500, she must be terrific."*

*"Leather jacket? Hmmm. Leather is expensive. He must be terrific."*

But that's all just part of the game. In reality, you already *are* terrific. In case you think you might not be, just remember that now, with DNA testing, we know that *you* are absolutely one of a kind in the universe. The time in which you exist is also just a flicker of an eyelash in eternity. So both you and the moment of your existence are among the rarest things there are. That makes you pretty goddamn terrific, if you ask me.

Now, back to the game. Your reputation precedes the money. Since this is partly a game of credits, your credits help create your reputation. Your credits are the answer to these questions: Oh, you're an actor? What have you done? Who're you with? (Who are you with—meaning, Who's your agent?)

Any good actor will rehearse and rehearse and rehearse. Here's something else for you to throw into the mix. Your answer to What have you done? can make a huge difference in what kind of jobs you get. You should figure out the strongest way of relaying your credits and practice saying that.

I once asked a girl, who had been complaining about her career being in the dumper, what she had done, and she answered, "Nothing."

I responded, "Well, you must have done something if you actually have a career that's in the dumper."

She said, "Well, in *The Godfather*, I was the girl whom Sonny humped up against the door on the day of his sister's wedding. But that was nothing. And in *The French Connection*, I was the lady with the baby buggy, but that was nothing. And I did a Hertz commercial and was on camera during the whole commercial, but I only got that because they wanted someone with a North Carolina accent, and I'm from North Carolina."

If you will let your credits be nothing, so will everyone else. But with three major credits like that, she should have stated them like they were golden, which they were.

I will add, though, that John Erwin, the former voice of Morris the Cat and other great accounts, was often asked what he had done. He would say, "Nothing. Nobody ever hires me."

He would do it with such scorn for the question that the asker would respond by saying something like, "Oh I get it! You do so much that I should have known what you do and not asked the question." That was an actual conversation I overheard.

That's a gutsy way of handling it, but then John has always been a gutsy guy.

As I began developing my own reputation, a young studio engineer, after meeting me, asked, "You're one of the top ten guys in the business, aren't you?"

Now I knew that there were lots of guys who made more money than I did, and more who had been around longer than me, and many who I thought were possibly more talented. So, was I in the top ten?

I said, "Gee, I don't know. Am I?"

"Oh, what's this, the old Mr. Humble act?" he asked.

"No," I said, "I mean, what if I'm only number eleven?"

He thought that was a great answer.

I thought, *"If you want me to be in the top ten, then I'll be in the top ten."*

People will let you be anything you say you are. They have no reason to think otherwise until you demonstrate that you are not what you say you are. So make it good.

If you did a Budweiser commercial for a local distributor, and I ask you what you have done, you can say simply that you did a Budweiser commercial. If you stop there, I'll let it be national. But if you give me more information and diminish the job, I'll let you do that, too.

Once in a while, I've been asked to be the guest hotshot at voice-over classes. When I find someone who has never worked for money, I will call that person up to the mic. We'll record something together like a Ford commercial, and then I'll hand the person a quarter.

"Now you're a professional," I'll say. "You've done it for money. That's it. So if somebody asks what you have done, you can tell them you just did a Ford spot with Jack Angel."

That is the unvarnished truth.

If you stop there, the person with whom you are speaking will let it be a Ford spot instead of a workshop event. Unless, of course the person you're talking to just happens to be connected to the Ford account. But, hey! How often can *that* happen?

Your agent is part of your credits, too. When I started in voice-over, there were only commercial agents and theatrical agents. Places such as William Morris and ICM didn't have voice-over departments.

I had been at The Ann Wright Agency when Bob Lloyd ran its voice department. The agency was well known in New York but was relatively new to Los Angeles. When I was asked who my agent was, and I replied it was Bob Lloyd at Ann Wright, most people would say something like, "Who else do they represent?"

When I mentioned a few people, the response would be, "Oh yeah. They have some good people."

Then I moved to Carey, Phelps & Colvin, which was a little better known, and people would say, "They have some darn good people."

When I moved to Cunningham & Associates, which was one of the top-two commercial agencies at the time, people would say, "Wow, they have all the best people in town."

So in about six months' time I went from being "good" to "darn good" to one of "the best people in town," just by changing agents. My talent hadn't changed a bit.

# SPEAKING OF AGENTS ...

Do you know why agents get only 10 percent?

Because that's all they're worth. *Ka-boom chuck!*

Your relationship with your agent is very important. Obviously your agent has to like you and like your work and remember what you do. But if your agent represents five hundred actors, you're entitled to about one five-hundredth of his or her time. If you rely on your agent to push and promote you, it's going to be a long, slow process. *You* can devote 100 percent of your time to further your career. The word "business" in the term "show business" is there because it *is* a business, and you should learn to treat it as such.

When you are given a time for an audition, show up early enough to look over the script ahead of time. Keep in touch with your agent's office by carrying a cell phone and keeping it turned on. Sometimes things happen fast in voice-over. Often there are only a few hours to set up, audition, and deliver a project. If you are right for it, but unavailable, you lose.

Also, if you create some new voice that you want your agency to remember for future auditions, get a copy of the spot and take it in and play it for them. Tell these folks how great it turned out and how happy the producers were, so you can embed this into your agent's memory as a huge positive.

Here are a few dos and don'ts when it comes to agents.

- Do keep your appointments. Audition slots are valuable, and usually an agency will have more qualified actors for that particular audition than times available.

- Don't go away or make yourself unavailable without booking out. That is, tell your agent when you'll be unavailable and when you'll be back. Nothing bothers agents more than to put you up for an audition, only to find that you're out of town or at a doctor's appointment.

- Do stay available, but don't bug the office all the time. Becoming a pest is the last thing you want to do. Your agent is working on your behalf.

- Don't discuss with your fellow actors all the jobs for which you have read. They will call their agents and ask to be submitted on your project, diminishing your chances of winning by however many more people get in on the auditions.

- Do discuss with your fellow actors what *they've* been reading on so you can tell your agent what's going on, just in case your agent hasn't heard about that particular project.

- Don't sign contracts unless you know what you're signing. AFTRA and SAG contracts are fairly simple, and you should become familiar with them. You should know the terms of the deal your agent made with the producers so that when you sign the contract the money is right. If it isn't, and you sign it, "Tough titty, said the kitty."

- Do carry your appointment book or PDA, (portable digital assistant) at all times, and refer to it often. I know that may sound odd, but I know of actors who missed auditions, and even jobs, because they forgot when they were and didn't bother checking their appointment book (yes, I've done it, too).

- Don't overestimate your abilities. You are not right for everything, in spite of what your mother says. I read for a project once where, at the top of the page, Alan Barzman was mentioned as a prototype. "Barz" was a good friend and had hired me many times. (In addition to being a radio producer, he was also a famous voice-over artist. Remember the Energizer Bunny spots that went on and on and on? That droning voice was Barzman's.) So I broke my own rule and called him and told him about the audition. His agent contacted the production company and asked if they'd like to have the *real* Alan Barzman read their copy. They were elated to have him read for the part. Unfortunately, the word came back that he was "not right" for the job. See? Even when you're the prototype, sometimes you're not right by whatever standard has been set.

- Do carry your résumé and demo CD with you to all sessions and auditions. You'd be surprised at how often you have an opportunity to hand them out to someone who may be of help to you.

- Don't accept jobs at home. Have them call your agent. T. J. Escott, one of the owners of CED (formerly Cunningham & Associates) used to remind me: "When a producer calls you at home, even though it may seem like it, he is not your friend. He wants something free or extra, or doesn't want to pay the ten percent commission, or any number of other things."

I learned the hard way about taking jobs without my agent's involvement. Some years ago, I was the announcer for the Pepsi Challenge radio spots on the West Coast. The advertising agency asked me to do a freebie for them. They were pitching a grocery chain and wanted me to voice one of their spots. I was glad to do it.

When I got to the studio, there was another actor in the booth doing another spot, and she wasn't cutting it. The producer asked me if I'd mind replacing her. He said that she was getting a demo fee and he would gladly pay me the same for doing over that spot. I did it. Everybody was happy.

The agency got the account and then wanted me to do some commercials for half of my normal fee. When my agents told them no, they were pissed off at me.

"After all we've done for you, how dare you?" Blah, blah, blah.

But get this: on the day they asked me to work for nothing, they were paying someone else to do a similar spot. Each member of the agency staff was getting paid, the studio was getting paid, and the engineer was getting paid. I was the only one who apparently didn't *deserve* to get paid that day. What had I done to be so unworthy? And then, once they got the account using my voice, we asked for my regular fee for the subsequent commercials and I went from being a hero to a schmuck. It all happened because I took that call at home.

And I was never asked to work for that agency again.

But I have a healthy outlook about it. I had learned early on that one small creative house didn't like me for some reason or another. And although I would have preferred that it not be that way, there wasn't anything I could do about it. At that same time, I realized that I had never yet worked for J. Walter Thompson, then the largest advertising agency in the world, and I was doing quite well without them. So if I never worked for that small production company either, so what? Besides, that comany went out of business a long time ago and I'm still here. I win!

## MORE MAGIC: *TRIANGLES*

There once was a brilliant scientist named R. Buckminster Fuller. He's the guy generally given credit for developing the geodesic dome. The Cinerama Dome Theater in Hollywood is a geodesic dome. So is the huge silver "golf ball" structure at Disney World. "Bucky" said he never created anything of the sort. He said he just played with triangles and discovered that if you link enough equilateral triangles together, they don't lie flat, they form a ball. He went on to prove scientifically that the basic building block of nature is the equilateral triangle. It's the strongest structure known to mankind. I'll show you that a little later.

Every year or so back then, atop Mount Wilson in Los Angeles, weather instruments got blown away when huge windstorms occurred. Fuller suggested they put all the equipment inside a geodesic dome. He was laughed at.

The experts said, "That flimsy little thing wouldn't last five minutes in all the wind that whips across the mountaintop."

So Bucky built a dome right next to all the weather instruments, and during the next big blow, all the weather gear was blown away, but the dome remained. Weather instruments on Mount Wilson are now inside a geodesic dome.

At any rate, Fuller said that one of the unique things about equilateral triangles is that they tend to want to remain equilateral. So if you extend one side, the other two sides automatically stretch to maintain the integrity of the triangle.

*"Aha!" says I. "There's the synergy! There are three ways to be an actor. Stage, screen, and radio. Or, live, film/tape, and voice. And one supports the other supports the other."*

Once I played Abraham Lincoln in a Kentucky Fried Chicken TV commercial for the Presidents Day giveaway of cherry pies. Abe was to lament the fact that they give pies away for George's birthday but not for his. At that time, I was younger and a bit thinner, and with the proper makeup and beard I had a similar look to Lincoln. When I was auditioning for the role, another guy walked in who was the rail splitter incarnate. He was tall, had the beard and the mole, his hair was right, and I thought he was a shoo-in. I was astounded when the producer, Ross McCanse, called and booked me for the spot.

"But Abe was there!" I insisted.

"Yes," Ross said, "but his voice was like Elmer Fudd's."

I got the part because I not only looked right for the part but sounded right as well. So my live/stage audition helped get me the screen/tape commercial, and the voice/radio clinched it. One supports the other supports the other.

(Looking back at that experience, it is clear that I was the better choice for another reason: The pie was small. In the hands of a huge Lincoln, it would have looked even smaller. Since I was not that big, I made the pie look bigger.)

Okay. Here's the deal about triangles.

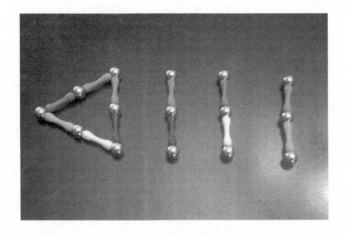

Those are two equilateral triangles. One is together and the other is not.

This shows two equilateral triangles, one added to the other. Except, one side is wasted. Nature would never waste a side, so it would add them together three dimensionally as in Figure 3.

Now, count the triangles. There is the base, and three sides, for a total of four triangles. One and one equals four. How powerful is that? When it comes to triangles, nothing is stronger. And a structure like this one is virtually indestructible.

If you triangulate acting, there are three ways to be an actor. You pay, you get paid, and you do it for free. The hardest part is to have to pay. Pictures, tapes, classes, parking, costumes—all that stuff is what you dole out your hard-earned cash for. Next easiest is to get money in return for the acting you like to do. The easiest is doing it for free: auditions, workshops, classes, anytime and everywhere. You're an actor. Act!

And remember Bucky's comment that if one side of a triangle extends, so do the other two sides?

It will extend its other two sides so as to remain equilateral.

The more you extend one side, the larger the triangle gets.

Now, consider your personal ratio of auditions to jobs—perhaps it is one out of twenty. So if you audition forty times, you get two jobs. Double the "do it free" side, and the "you get money" side doubles too. Then, if you discover you're not hitting in a certain category, you can take classes to improve so that you now start getting more of those jobs. Double the "you pay" side and the "you get money" side doubles too. But now you're getting more auditions in that difficult category, and now you're better at it, so maybe your ratio changes to one out of ten. Putting effort on any side of the triangle forces the other two sides to grow proportionately. Put effort on two sides and the triangle quadruples. Since the easiest side is the "do it free" side, just have fun doing it and your career will soar.

Do it for the right person and you could make a fortune.

Bud Davis is an example of how someone can re-invent himself from agent to voice talent. I first became aware of him when he ran the voice-over department at Cunningham & Associates. Bud had great charisma.

On one occasion, when I walked into Bell Sound Studios, the lobby was filled with actors, but one person was dominating the room. He was a tall, good-looking, stylish gentleman, with a deep voice and a commanding presence. I asked who he was and was told it was Bud Davis. Bud had more dynamism than any of the actors in the room.

Bud eventually left Cunningham and produced a couple of low-budget movies, but when that didn't become productive, he decided to try his hand at voice-over. His voice was much like Danny Dark's, and ironically, they were both from Oklahoma.

Arlene Thornton represented Bud when she ran the voice department at Abrams, Rubaloff & Lawrence. One day, Bud told me that he just wasn't hitting any of the auditions except the straight announcer spots, and he asked me whether he should give up trying on the others. I told him to take an animation workshop with Michael Bell, who was not only a terrific voice actor but also conducted an animation class. On top of that, he directed animation. I was in *Peter Pan and the Pirates*, a sixty-five-episode series, and Michael directed many of the episodes.

Bud already knew Michael, as they had both been at the Cunningham agency previously. In fact, Michael attributed his success in the business to Bud's actions while running the voice-over department there. I said, "Michael loves you. He'll be kind to you, and he's a great teacher."

Bud signed up the next day. All he wanted was to become more adept at doing two-voice spots … those husband-and-wife things, or doctor-patient commercials.

A week or so later, he called me and said I had really put him in a pickle, because his assignment that week was to learn how to do a British accent.

"What do I do now, pal?" he asked.

"Rent *My Fair Lady*," I said.

I assume he did, because when I heard his new demo tape a month later, Bud had mastered all of it.

He took his tape to Wally Burr, the director of such animation shows as *G.I. Joe*, *The Transformers*, *Gem & the Holograms*, and many others, and asked Wally to critique it. Wally liked what he heard so much that he hired Bud to do voices on both *G.I. Joe* and *The Transformers*. Bud more than doubled his income.

Suggesting renting a movie to learn an accent reminds me of another technique for doing the same thing. I did a series of TV shows produced by an Italian, Bruno Vailati, who shot stories about sponge divers, coral divers, and other men of the sea. Bruno spoke several languages. He had learned English in England, and his Italian accent also was laced with a British accent. Bruno hired seamen of various nationalities to crew the ships while filming—Spaniards, Italians, Englishmen, Greeks—and he spoke all the languages. So, for the American audiences, he had to loop anyone who didn't speak English.

My then-agent Bob Lloyd handed me a script and said, "There are two Greeks in this episode. One is seventy-five years old and the other forty-five. Your audition is tomorrow, so get familiar with the material."

I protested, "I don't do a Greek accent. My father is Greek, but I never tried the accent. I can't do it."

"Go home and study the script. You can do it," was his reply.

I took home the script and looked at it and said, "Okay, my father has said all these words, just not in this order."

So I listened as if I was hearing him read the script, and sure enough, there it was.

At the audition, I said I was there to read for both parts, and Bruno replied, "The old Greek is seventy-five years old. You can't do him."

"Can I try?" I asked.

His body language became very closed off as I started reading. After a couple of sentences, though, he came out of the chair, almost yelling. "That's him! I don't know how you did that, but that's him!"

I got both roles.

By the way, there seem to be people who can do accents and "funny voices" and those who can't. I've always thought it was just like there are people who can throw a basketball through a hoop and those who can't. The ones who can are the ones who practice. You should be able to do—with your vocal mechanism—everything anyone else can do. You just need to practice and play with the mechanics of doing voices and *listen!*

But let's get back to the triangles. The thing about the triangle is this: Your life is not made up of just one triangle. It's a whole ball. It's a geodesic ball, more like the structure you see here.

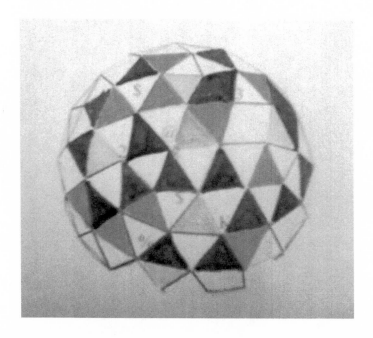

And since it's made up of triangles, if you extend one side of one triangle, the whole ball expands exponentially. It gets huge. Everything in your life expands if you just cause one side of one triangle to grow. Cause two or three sides to expand at the same time and you might become Donald Trump. (Just do something about the hair.)

# Be My Valentine!

So I was out of radio, doing voice-overs and having a great time. One day I went into the office of Alan Barzman, one of the best writer/producers of radio spots in Hollywood, who was opening the day's mail. When he got to an envelope that contained a demo tape from an announcer, he tossed it into the trash and said, "Gee, just what I need! Another demo tape from someone I don't know."

"Barz" had been around a while and knew almost every talented voice actor in town. He knew what they could and couldn't do, and he knew what he had to do to get out of them the performance he wanted. His attitude was, why should I waste my time listening to someone I don't know and who is probably lousy anyway?

In that moment, for me, he became Everyman. I was about to mail my own demo tape to a thousand producers all over the nation, and I thought, *"Damn! I'm going to send out all these tapes and they're all going to wind up in someone's trash."*

So that presented the puzzle that needed to be answered. How do you get someone who doesn't want to listen to your tape to *want* to listen to your tape (now a CD)?

When I was in radio, an astoundingly good San Francisco radio station was KSFO. The morning man was a Bay Area legend named Don Sherwood. He and program director Al Newman merged their creative minds and came up with some terrific promotions, one of which was "KSFO Loves You" bumper stickers. These things were seen all over San Francisco, Oakland, and points north, south, and east. I thought it was the best radio off-air promotion I had ever seen.

Now that I was out of radio, I somehow had to promote myself as a voice-over artist in a business awash with good announcer/actors. How could I get a thousand producers to *want* to listen to my tape?

I didn't know how to promote a person, but I did know how to promote a radio station. So, I made *me* the station. Rosemary Deasy, an artist friend of mine, created a valentine poster for me. It had 110 red hearts with gold frames all around each of them. In the center was a drawing of me, looking much like the kid on the Cracker Jack box, and I was holding a big red heart in which were written the words "Jack Angel Loves You."

Rosemary had painstakingly created one of the most fabulous valentines I had ever seen.

The thing about valentines is that when we were kids, we all got them and loved getting them. As we grew older, for the most part, valentines stopped coming. So if you get a valentine as an adult, you are sort of transformed into that child again, with warm, fuzzy feelings about the person who sent it—even if you don't know who it is. (Remember the ones you got from Guess Who?)

During my eighteen years in radio, I saw that when folded promotional posters were sent to us disc jockeys, we never put them up on the wall when they had creases in them. But if those posters came to us in mailing tubes—thus without creases—we always put them up on the wall, regardless of the content.

So I had one thousand valentines printed. I rolled them into tubes and then mailed them to commercial producers all over the country. I imagined that even though there were around two hundred producers who already knew me or knew about me, eight hundred others would look at the poster and ask, "Who the hell is Jack Angel? And why does he love me? Do I know him? Am I supposed to know him?"

People don't like to have unanswered questions rattling around in their heads. They will go to any lengths to find the answers to those questions. I even pictured one guy bringing my poster into the next office and asking that person, "Who is this guy? Do we know him?" About a week later, a demo tape would arrive, and it would be the answer to some of his questions. *"Ah! That guy who sent me the valentine is a voice actor."*

But that doesn't answer the question Do I know him and am I supposed to know him? Of course, listening to the tape might answer both questions. I didn't care *why* they listened—I thought my tape was so terrific that producers couldn't help but be impressed with it once they heard it.

Well, did it work for me?

Shortly after my tapes went out, a producer from Saint Louis came to town to record some spots for Anheuser-Busch beer. His agency was trying to land the account with a series of funny radio spots. When I auditioned for him, he remembered the valentine and said, "Man, I got this valentine and it said 'Jack Angel Loves You,' and I wondered, 'Who the hell is Jack Angel?' And then Charlie, in the next office, came in with his poster and asked if I knew who this was."

This was just as I had envisioned; it took all my efforts to keep from bursting out loud with laughter. And then he went on, "By the way, your demo tape was great!"

He told me that he was going to cast in the morning and record in the afternoon, so I should stay in touch with my agent. He said he had the whole town to choose from and he would hire me for *one* spot, and that nobody would do more than one. I did work for him that afternoon, and of all the brilliant radio actors in Hollywood, I was the only one who was on *two* spots. That didn't quite pay for the whole promotion, but it came damn close.

Shortly after that, I got in on another audition, and the producer said, "You sent me something really funny. What was it?"

His assistant said, "It was the valentine."

"Oh yes!" he said. "That's why you're here."

During that period, it was not unusual for actors to go to various advertising agencies to audition. Most of the agencies had in-house recording studios for just such a purpose. As I traveled around Hollywood auditioning, I saw my valentine posters all over town on the walls of producers' offices. Someone from Bell Sound Studios called me and asked for another one. It seems that people were stealing them right off the walls.

One time as I walked into another recording studio, the lobby was filled with my peers, who were discussing the valentine and how talented I was. Now I had *them* doing my PR! Word of mouth is the best advertising, especially when it's being done by your competitors.

Danny Dark, who at the time was the voice of NBC, had lunch with me at the old Hollywood Athletic Club. On our way out after lunch, we ran into George Suski, a producer of TV promos and trailers. George said, "I'm really pissed off at you. That valentine you created was the best personal promotional piece I've ever seen in this town, and I didn't get one."

"George," I said, "you were on my mailing list. I don't know why you didn't get one. I've got some in my car. Do you want one?"

"Yeah!" he said enthusiastically. After reaching my car, I gave George a poster. All Danny could do was stand with his mouth agape in utter amazement.

Yeah, it worked, on a whole lot of levels.

And that year, my income almost doubled.

By the way, some contemporaries of mine decided to promote themselves in similar fashion. Mark Elliot, who for several years was a promo announcer at CBS and still does a lot of work for Disney, had a poster made to look like a big dart board with his face in the bull's eye. The poster read, "When you want a voice that hits the mark, shoot for Mark Elliot." In his rolled-up presentation, he included a dart.

Dave Hull, "The Hullabalooer," had a jigsaw puzzle made which, after you put all the pieces in place, said, "Puzzled over what voice to use for your next project? Let Dave Hull put it together for you."

# MORE PROMOTIONAL IDEAS

As long as we're on the subject of promotions, here are some examples of other ideas that seem to have worked.

Robert Ringer wrote a book called *Winning through Intimidation*, which was on the bestsellers list for several months. He was a hot-shot real estate salesperson who would put buyer and seller together in hopes of reaping a large commission after the sale of a big office building. Unfortunately for him, every time he would get near to closing the deal, the buyer and seller would consummate the deal themselves and screw him out of his commission. They'd say things such as "Who needs you? You're just another real estate salesman." After he heard the same thing three times, he realized that they were right. He *was* just "another salesman." It was then that he vowed never to hear those words again.

The next time he put a deal together, he went in with an entourage. Everything had a flourish to it. He even created what he called a five-dollar brochure. The upshot of the whole thing was that in every deal after that, he got his commission. The principals in the deal thought that he must be quite special and that down the line they might need him again.

I never really got past that point in Ringer's book, because it occurred to me that I was just another voice-over guy, and what I needed was my own "five-dollar brochure." At that time, we were using five-inch reel-to-reel tapes for our demos (later to be replaced by cassette tapes and then CDs). Everyone had a single tape with a cute label, and they all looked alike. It was the "brochure" of the voice actor.

I decided to make two tapes—one a commercial tape, the other character and animation. I designed an outer box in which both tapes would be contained. Since I wanted to make the whole thing really stand out, I hired a printer, who used gold-leaf lettering on black matte covers on all three boxes so as to look like jewelry on black felt. Each unit was slightly more than five dollars—gold leaf is expensive—and I had one thousand of them made.

As costly as it was (and the postage jacked up the cost even more), the result was just what I wanted: spectacular! I know I got one job just from the packaging alone. A Century City agency was putting on its dog-and-pony show for a client, so they brought a bunch of tapes into the conference room to play for him. The client said, "I want to hear the guy in the gold box." He was already predisposed to like me because he knew packaging, and if I could afford a gold box, I must be terrific. I got the job, and again, it almost paid for the whole project.

The other advantage of having a double-sized box is that it stands out among the other slim boxes when all are placed on a shelf in a producer's office. The only thing visible is the spine of the box. I always urged friends to make the print clear and large so it could be seen from across the room. With a double-sized spine, my name stood out like a shining gold beacon.

In show business also there is the "save their asses" syndrome, as with Robert Ringer's "We may need him down the line." I was acquainted with a writer-producer of a major television series. He said that when they audition an actor who's not right for the part, but who may be the kind of person who could possibly save their asses down the line, they will often give the actor a crumb or two or at least save the audition for future reference.

I've always felt that you should sink some money into your career every once in a while, either by taking classes, or sending out tapes, or both. If the president of General Motors was considering using you as a spokesperson for, say, Cadillac, and said, "I'm about to invest over $100,000 in your career," and then asked, "How much have you spent on it lately?" you ought to have good answer.

Every time I spent money on me, it came back tenfold.

My first radio job was at KYOS in Merced, California. Merced was a one-station town until Joe Gamble opened Radio KWIP, a small daytime "coffee pot" with only 250 watts of power. Just before the station went on the air, Joe sent a letter to every merchant in town—somewhere between fifty and one hundred—that said, "Radio KWIP in going on the air May 1st, and it means profits for you as an advertiser. And just to prove it, here's the first dollar."

The beauty of that promotion was that when his salespeople went calling, they were the ones who had given the merchant a buck. What an icebreaker. Radio KWIP did very well commercially.

I had always been planning to use that idea as a way to promote myself, when a friend and I were talking about how to get his career off the ground. I told him about Radio KWIP. I envisioned he'd have checks printed with the promotional stuff on the stub. If you want to promote to advertising people, you're promoting to the most creative promotional minds in the world, so your promotion had better be as good and creative as possible. Well, this friend of mine missed part of the message. Instead, he wrote checks out of his personal account and included a note that read, "I know you're busy, so here's a dollar to listen to my demo tape."

It met with mixed reviews. Some people were delighted with it, but a few were somehow insulted. He actually got a few very good gigs as a direct result of the mailing, but at least one agency executive returned the check and the tape with a terse note that said, "If you're so awful you have to bribe people to listen to your tape, I want no part of you." That guy probably wasn't very creative, anyway. I think he over-reacted, but the message was clear: Do it right or don't do it at all.

I won the role of a plumber on a radio spot a few years ago because the woman in charge of casting heard my voice on the audition and said, "When I heard your voice, I saw butt crack." I put together my "butt crack" demo with a string of blue collar voices I had done over the past couple of years and my agent emailed it to radio casting directors with a note explaining why it was being sent.

Sometimes it just takes a note from your agent to get someone to want to listen to your tape. Arlene Thornton, president of Arlene Thornton & Associates, a major commercial talent agency in Los Angeles, is asked quite often to describe the person on the tape so as to generate interest. Once, when she represented a woman whose voice was strong and who needed something to inspire people to listen to her demo, Arlene wrote simply: "If God was a woman, this is what she would sound like." If you got that note with a tape, wouldn't you listen to see what God sounds like?

Another client was Alan Barzman's son, Christopher, when he was about eighteen years old. Arlene wrote, "Unless you're looking for the perfect teen voice, DON'T listen to this tape. Save it for the right moment and the right project." Chris got two or three jobs after that mailing.

Along the way, Arlene has done several great promotions for her agency. One that really stands out occurred when a new production company announced its opening. She bought a portable cassette player, put one of her house tapes inside, and sent it over with a note that simply read, "Press PLAY."

Another promotional idea worth mentioning also came from those fertile minds at KSFO in San Francisco. They ran a newspaper ad for Don Sherwood, who did voices of a variety of characters on his deejay show. The ad included a drawing of Don, standing in his underwear, and beside him were paper doll cutouts of various costumes for his radio characters. Normally, the best you can expect from a newspaper ad is that it is read once and then the page is turned. Readers were cutting this one out and playing with it. In a case like that, it worked again and again. I have never seen this type of promotion done by anyone else, and I always thought it would be a natural for an on-camera character actor … not necessarily as a newspaper ad (that can get a little expensive) but as a poster to be sent around to various casting directors. It could also work for a voice actor.

There's a fine line between promotional calls, sending material, and becoming a pest. Lots of actors under-promote, and a few promote to excess. The line is so individual for everyone that you just have to use your own judgment and hope you don't cross the line.

Speaking to a group of people in which a talent agent was present, I offered my views on personal promotions. She reacted by saying, "If I represented you and you did things like that, I'd release you."

And I said, "If I had you as an agent and you felt that way, I'd fire you."

In the late 1970s, some brave folks published a magazine for the commercial broadcasting production industry called *Commercials Monthly*. For their third-anniversary issue, I bought an ad in the magazine congratulating them. I think the only thing I accomplished with this ad was to demonstrate to the voice-over actors who bought the magazine that I had a little money to blow. And even though I continued to buy ads in industry publications to congratulate production companies and producers for one thing or another, it's my opinion that ads like this only make money for the magazine and don't do much to further one's career.

## JACK ANGEL

# Damn! He Forgot!

A scary aspect of the whole promotional business is that as human beings we forget. Early in my voice-over career, my agent was Bob Lloyd. He later became known as "The Voicecaster,", and his was the first casting company to concentrate solely on voice auditions.

Bob made an appointment with the creative director of a major advertising agency in Hollywood (we'll call him Jim) to play tapes of some of his people. Bob led off with mine.

Jim said, "I don't want to waste time listening to Jack's tape. I'm a big fan of his and I listen to him on the radio."

Bob then played a couple of other tapes. In those days, demo tapes would have two or three entire spots strung together, and you had to listen a whole minute to one of them before getting to the next. Mine, however, was different. I had clipped ten or fifteen seconds of each spot, and I went from straight to character to crazy to straight, and so on. Seizing the moment, Bob asked Jim to listen to my tape to see if he liked the way it was constructed. Not only did Jim love the arrangement, but also he said, "Boy, am I glad you had me listen to Jack's tape. I had no idea he did all those voices. I thought he was just an announcer."

Jim was genuinely impressed. A week later, however, when Jim called Bob to cast another project, he relayed the specs for the voice he wanted. Bob suggested he use me, to which Jim responded, "No, I don't want an announcer—I want a character voice."

Another time, I worked for Pancho Maxume, who produced promotional spots for record albums. After the session I gave him my demo reel, and as it was playing, people from offices near the studio came in to listen. Everyone seemed very impressed; many remarked about it. "Is that all one guy?" "Wow!" "Amazing."

A week or two later, I was told to call Pancho to audition over the phone for a new project. When I told him my name, it was clear that he didn't remember who I was. He asked if I'd ever done a record promotion spot before. When I reminded him of our last meeting, he said, "Oh, Jack! Right! I'm sorry, I forgot. You'll do fine." I got the job.

But the point is people forget ... even when they're really impressed. They forget. So perhaps a little reminder from time to time is in order. A personal promotional piece should do the trick.

Agents, too, are not immune to memory lapses. Shortly after I signed with Carey, Phelps & Colvin, a talent agency that no longer exists, there was a commercial project involving a lot of funny voice impersonations. Many of the voices were ones I was really good at performing—Humphrey Bogart, Peter Lorre, that sort of thing. When I heard the spots on the radio and heard some of CPC's clients, I asked Bob Colvin if there was a reason I had not been included in the auditions. Had I alienated the producers? Was there something else wrong?

Bob told me, "I'm sorry. It wasn't you; I just forgot all about you."

I thought about this. If he could forget me in an area in which I felt I was the strongest, what chance would I have in areas where I might not be the obvious choice? After all, I had just signed with CPC and frequently was in and out of their offices—signing contracts, discussing my pictures and tapes and my place in the scheme of things there, and doing all the other things that one does when in a new relationship with an agency. How in the hell could he forget me?

I had to seek representation elsewhere. That's when I went to Cunningham.

# THE VALUE OF POSITIONING

I was at Cunningham & Associates for an audition one day. Rita Venari—who later became a partner in the agency Sutton, Barth and Venari—was on the phone with a producer who was seeking someone who could do a great French accent. As I walked toward her desk, Rita looked up at me and then said into the phone, "Well, there's Jack Angel, and ah ..." She had to think of who else did a French accent. The pause set me apart from the rest.

Later that day, I went by the *Voicecaster* to see Bob Lloyd, and as the fates would have it, that same producer was on the phone with Bob at the very moment I walked in, asking the same question she had asked Rita. As I walked toward him, Bob said, "Well, there's Jack Angel."

He went on to list other players who did French accents. It turned out that the producer hired Bob to handle the auditions, and he placed me first on the tape.

Not only had both Bob and Rita mentioned me first, but also it sounded to the producer as if there was this one guy in all of Hollywood who did a great French accent, and then there was everybody else. With my positioning on the tape as the first, there was no way I wasn't going to get the job.

I realized then and there that how you are positioned can be quite important.

Another time, T. J. Escott called me to tell me about a voice gig I had been hired for on his recommendation. It was for an old and wise man with an "authentic" Chinese accent. I said, "T. J., I don't do an authentic Chinese accent … I do a poor imitation of Charlie Chan."

He said, "Just go. Don't worry about it."

I went, but I did worry about it. And when I recorded my "authentic Charlie Chan" lines, the producers were thrilled. They even called T. J. to thank him.

In order to improve your positioning you must remember to promote with your own agents. Take them to lunch once in a while. Send flowers or take a basket of fresh fruit with you when you are called into the office.

# VISUALIZE YOUR WAY TO SUCCESS

During my time in radio, I spent four and a half years at KEX in Portland, Oregon. I was the afternoon drive-time disc jockey.

I knew I was pretty good, but it wasn't until I went on vacation in 1967 that I discovered just how good I was. I had driven from Maine to Oregon, listening to the great radio disc jockeys in all the major cities on the way. These guys were legends of the air waves in New York, Boston, Philadelphia, and Chicago. What I realized was that on my worst day, I was better and more entertaining than most of the guys I listened to. About a week after I was back on the air at KEX, my program director, Mark Blinoff, said to me, "Man! I don't know what happened to you on vacation, but you have never sounded better."

And I guess he was right.

I had just finished reading *The Magic of Believing*, by Claude Bristol, the book that comedian Phillis Diller credited with helping to jump start her career. The book instructed that part of the key to success in any venture is to visualize yourself in that position. I decided that I was ready for Los Angeles. L.A. was the big time.

I wanted to move to KMPC, the best of the best, the flagship of Golden West Broadcasters. Owned by Gene Autry, Golden West was the dominant radio organization on the West Coast, with stations in Los Angeles, San Francisco (KSFO), Portland (KEX), and Seattle (KVI).

Accordingly, I typed the words KMPC LOS ANGELES on small pieces of paper, which I stuck to various things so I'd see them throughout the day. They were on the dashboard of my car, across from where I sat at the breakfast table, on the mirror where I shaved, and even at KEX, in front of me when I did my show. They were constant reminders for me to visualize myself at KMPC. The process started in mid-October. By February 2, I had been hired and was on the air at KMPC. This had taken just three and a half months.

There are a lot of books on visualization. In addition to *The Magic of Believing*, *Psycho-Cybernetics* has had a profound effect on me. This book discussed an experiment in which they split a basketball team into two parts. One practiced free throws on a court and the other sat in a room and visualized practice. The second group's rate of improvement was almost the same as the first group's.

Remembering how well visualizing worked, later when I was a freelancer doing voice-overs, I wanted my income to take a giant leap upward. So I made a graph on which I marked a pencil line at the dollar amount I wanted to reach. I concentrated on getting that graph to obey my demand. Wouldn't you know it? By the time the year was up, my income total was right at the point I had drawn on the paper.

I said to myself, *"You dumb ass! You should have put the spot higher!"*

Charlie Adler, a young actor from Nyack, New York, replaced Harvey Fierstein in *Torch Song Trilogy* on Broadway. Until then, Harvey, who was also the playwright, had played the role. I asked Charlie how he won the part and he said, "When I left Nyack on the train I told myself I was a light bulb which would get brighter and brighter the closer I got to New York City. And when I stepped onto the stage for my audition, I was so bright I blinded everyone in the theater."

When Charlie went on the road with *Torch Song*, the company would wind up in Los Angeles, and that's where he decided to stay. He walked into Abrams/Rubaloff & Lawrence looking for representation. He said he was particularly interested in doing animation. He didn't have a tape, so Arlene Thornton, who was running the V.O. department, asked him to show her what he could do. He went into the studio, turned all the lights off, turned his back to the control booth and proceeded to blow Arlene away with his talent.

She agreed to represent Charlie and started sending him on animation auditions. Guest shots, series regulars, specials, whatever came up—And he got everything he auditioned for. He hit twelve straight. What a ratio that was.

He then auditioned for number thirteen. He called Arlene a few days later and asked about the job. "You didn't get it," she said.

After a long silence he responded, "What do you mean I didn't get it?"

"Well, Charlie," she said, "sometimes you don't get them." He was stunned.

Arlene and I have used visualization techniques for buying cars and houses, finding office space when there was none available, and lots of other things and events we wanted to happen. (Oh, did I fail to mention she and I are married to one another? Sorry!)

As long as we're visualizing, consider this. Most actors will tell you they just want to *work* and don't want to *play all the games* one has to play in order to get the work. *Work is good, games are bad.* It's hard to change the games into work, because nobody wants to heap more work on themselves. Athletes, on the other hand, want to get into the game and don't like having to do all the work to get into the game. *Games are good, work is bad.* Smart coaches turn all the exercising and practicing into games so it's easier to get the players interested. As an actor, if you just change the labels so they read like the athletes'—work is bad, games are good—you can then turn all those nasty work things into games so that you can now dance through life playing. Since there is ample evidence to show that life is just a game anyway, if you're not having fun, you're doing it wrong.

# THE LIGHT GOES ON!

It's interesting to look back at some of the twists and turns that get us from one place to the next.

My last radio gig was at KFI, in Los Angeles, before it became the talk-show-format station it is today. It was always referred to in those days as "the sleeping giant." KFI is a huge, 50,000-watt radio station that for many years was mismanaged into ratings oblivion. I worked there twice, under two sets of management. During my first stint in 1971, while we were finally kicking some butt in the ratings race, our esteemed manager went golfing with one of his cronies. During their game, the manager asked what the man thought of KFI's programming. The gent replied that he listened only to talk radio and that music radio was passé. Well, I swear to you, the next day, Mr. Genius held a staff meeting to announce his decision to turn the station into L.A.'s new talk outlet.

"Nobody is listening to music radio anymore," he said. "So on Monday morning, when you come to work, don't play any music; just start talking. Now don't be controversial, and don't insult motherhood or the flag," he urged. "And don't get into religion and stuff like that."

I asked, "Since we've been playing music all this time, what do we hang this sudden change on?"

"That's your problem," he responded.

I could see my whole career swirling down the toilet. So I said, "Well, your problem is this: I was hired to be a disc jockey, not a talk-show host. When I come to work Monday, I'll be playing music."

The room fell quiet. The other deejays looked like they were in shock.

Then the manager snorted back, "If you do, you won't have a future with KFI."

"If you go to a talk format," I replied, "I don't want a future with KFI."

It was kind of a gutsy thing to do, but at that moment that's exactly how I felt.

The station remained a music station. It wasn't until several years later, under yet another management team, that KFI finally reached its full potential as the talk station we now recognize.

There is a rule in the world that goes like this: when it's my turn to be boss, if you won't let me be boss, you can't play. Sure enough, when my contract at KFI was up, and even though my ratings were higher than they had ever been, I was fired. Professionally, it was the most devastating thing that had ever happened to me. I should have seen it coming but I didn't. I had thought that if the ratings were up and we were kicking some butt, naturally they would want to maintain the status quo, forgetting all about my screwing up their plans for a talk format. A huge negative had just invaded me.

Since I had a family with mouths to feed, I was forced to find another way of supporting them. I had already once overstayed my welcome at the other major "good music" station in town, KMPC, and I had no interest in becoming a "rock jock" again. So acting, and particularly voice acting, was the method I chose.

Three years later, Jack the Actor was cooking in voice-over. I was making twice as much money as I had ever made in radio, I had my weekends free, and I didn't have to go to any staff meetings and listen to some program director—who could never make it as a disc jockey—tell me how to conduct my show because I was doing it wrong. My professional life was perfect!

Then I heard me say to myself, *"Damn! Am I glad KFI fired me!"* When I realized what I had just said, I noticed that the worst thing had transformed itself into the best thing that ever happened—and in just a few years. I thought, *"Wow! If the worst thing just became the best, then all the other stuff I carry around as negatives must have also served to get me to this moment, and I just missed it."*

It is a matter of *now*—I reasoned to myself—and where I am at this moment is perfect. If *now* is perfect, then everything that *ever* happened, and everything that *never* happened, has helped get me to here, *now*.

What a revelation! All the "bad stuff" was really "good stuff." So I played a game with myself that went on for almost a year. As I drove from job to job, and from audition to audition, I rolled the videotape in my head to see past experiences. Every time I identified a "negative" in my life, I made myself find three ways that that event or person helped me get to *now*. Three positives to outweigh the one negative. In every case, I found at least three ways and sometimes more.

For example, while my acting success followed my being fired from KFI, I would not have originally had that gig at KFI had I not been fired first from my prior job at KMPC. The people at KMPC hadn't always want to fire me; they wanted me to spend the next three or four years rotting away on the all-night shift. They had promised, when I agreed to work their all-night show, that as soon as there was an opening elsewhere on the schedule, I would get that job. Of course, the program director who had made that promise was no longer at the station when the opening came. When it happened, Jim Lange was hired to fill it. So at that time, I held KMPC in high contempt.

Truth be told, working at KMPC gave me enormous credibility as a deejay and helped me improve my craft, which helped me get noticed by the program director of KFI. And getting fired from KMPC opened the door for me to move on. And so on and on. Once I transformed KMPC to a positive, I no longer suffered under the weight of carrying it around as a loss. And by the way, KMPC is long gone (so is that advertising agency that never hired me again) and I'm still here. Whoopee!

After about a year of transforming negatives to positives, I became bored with the game and stopped. But by then, there were very few negatives left in my past life. I felt as light as a feather.

Things still come up as negatives. The trick is to accept them as part of life's little surprises as quickly as possible and move on until you can transform them into positives. They are all part of the adventure.

# THERE AIN'T NO NEGATIVES
## (JUST SLANGY DOUBLE NEGATIVES)

As I sought to banish the negatives, I thought, *"Hmmm. There are NO negatives! Well, if that's true, how do I reconcile the fact that I audition maybe ten times before I get a job? Aren't all the auditions I didn't get negatives? NO, NO, NO!"*

First, when you get selected to audition, *you won.* All 110,000 members of AFTRA and SAG wanted to audition, and only you and a handful of others actually got in on the audition. That day, you were chosen to play at *world class* level. *You won.*

Second, you got the opportunity to practice your craft in a competitive audition before casting directors or a show's producer or director. If you weren't right for this job, maybe you would be right for something else they're working on. *You won.* And by the way, being "not right" for any job is totally subjective on the part of the producer. *It doesn't mean anything else.*

And third, you moved closer to *your* job. If your personal ratio of hits to auditions is, say, one out of twenty (and it isn't!), the faster you get though the other nineteen—those that are not yours—the faster you get to yours. *You won.* So, each time you *don't* get one, *you still win.*

Emmy winner Michael Imperioli, who played the part of Christopher Moltisanti on *The Sopranos*, said in an interview that he auditioned over 350 times before he ever got a job. But he hung in there and kept going back and going back.

I asked the great Ernie Anderson—who had been the promo voice of ABC for twenty or more years, and maybe the best announcer I ever heard—what the secret to his success was, and he said, "They call, I go."

Do you want some more positives? Okay:

- You got out of the house.

- You got to see your peers and chit-chat about all of your and their successes.

- You saw an old friend you'd almost forgotten.

- You heard a new joke. Or you heard an old joke you'd forgotten.

- You heard about another audition somewhere (because actors are always bragging about all the auditions they've been on) that you get to tell your agent about and maybe get in on.

Get the point? There are *no* negatives, unless, of course, you prefer to walk around under a dark cloud. Since the choice is yours, why not opt for positives? As Shakespeare wrote, "There is nothing either good or bad, but thinking makes it so."

A lot of times, you can kill yourself before you ever get started. When the audition is over, let it go. I had a friend who was single, talented, and as happy-go-lucky as a guy could get. He had the best times at auditions. If he hit one, okay, if not, he knew he'd get the next one, or the one after that.

When he got married, nothing changed until he became a father and his wife quit her job to be a stay-at-home mom. Now the weight of the whole family was on his shoulders, getting heavier and heavier. He went into auditions as if his very survival depended on his getting the job. The fun in his voice was replaced by angst. And somehow it went into the microphone, traveled onto the tape, out of the speakers, and into the producers' ears, and it was no longer what they were looking for. He couldn't just let the auditions go anymore. They all became too important.

A similar thing happens to people who begin to split their interests between acting and writing or acting and producing (or whatever else turns them on). When their heads are stuck in another project while they're actually trying to audition for a part in a commercial or a show, the distraction, although subtle, often takes away from their performances. When it comes out the other end, something is missing.

I don't mean to imply it's wrong to get involved in other projects or interests—just be aware that there are consequences to every action. Sometimes your actions in one area may serve to defeat you in others. By the same token, the result of your actions may be a synergy that is to your liking. Make sure your actions are leading to the results that you want.

Recently I went to see a performance by a friend of mine, world famous juggler Mark Nizer. Mark and I have known each other for fifteen or twenty years, but up until then I had never seen him perform. He was stunning. If Sir Isaac Newton were alive today he would complain that Mark defies the laws of gravity.

Mark has been a professional juggler for thirty years and won the title of "World's Greatest Juggler" with what he calls "the impossible trick." He spins a basketball on one finger and then kicks another ball on top of the spinning ball and this one spins in the opposite direction. It took him seven years to actually do the trick. He tried it every day for seven years until he got it right and then waited another five years perfecting it before he put it in his show. That's perseverance. What does it have to do with voice-overs? It has to do with perseverance and winning.

# Warming Up

While I said earlier that I would read billboards on the way to my radio gigs in order to warm up, there were other exercises I did as well.

Try saying this until you can say it fast with no mistakes:

Theopholis Thistle, the successful thistle sifter, in sifting a sieve full of un-sifted thistles, thrust three thousand thistles through the thick of his thumb. If Theopholis Thistle, the successful thistle sifter in sifting a sieve full of unsifted thistles thrust three thousand thistles through the thick of his thumb, see that thou in sifting a sieve full of unsifted thistles thrust not three thousand thistles through the thick of thy thumb.

Here're a few more:

Bill had a billboard. Bill also had a board bill. The board bill bored Bill, so Bill sold the billboard to pay the board bill. After Bill sold the billboard to pay the board bill, the board bill no longer bored Bill.

Betty Botter bought some butter. "But," she said, "this butter's bitter. If I put it in my batter, it will make my batter bitter. But a bit of better butter will but make my batter better." So Betty Botter bought a bit of better butter, put it in her bitter batter, thus Betty Botter made her bitter batter better.

The sea seethes as it recedes.

And the old favorite:

Peter Piper picked a peck of pickled peppers. A peck of pickled peppers, Peter Piper picked. (I always want to say "pickled peckers" but I restrain myself most of the time.)

There are a lot more tongue-twisters, and if you know some, use them.

Now you're almost ready to audition. But before you speak one word, you should analyze the copy to determine your approach. There are three ways to be a voice actor.

The first is to be who you are. Just be yourself. Talk the words as if you were talking to a friend.

Next, be slightly larger than life. Like if you're squeezing the Charmin. Who really squeezes toilet paper and then talks about it to someone? You have to add a dimension just above reality in order to make the copy believable.

Finally, there are cartoon voices and big network announcer voices. These are all very much larger than life. No human talks like Goofy. No "real person" sounds like the guys doing network promos for nighttime dramas: *CSI Miami! CBS Monday!*

Back in my radio days, I got so locked in to sounding like a radio announcer that I didn't realize I sounded that way when I spoke to people off the air. It took me quite a while to work my way back to sounding real when I needed to. When I started doing a lot of voice-overs, it was easier for me to create a "real person" character. For instance, when an announcer goes into Bob's Big Boy, he or she says, "I'll have a hamburger and a cup of coffee." Every word, every consonant pronounced exactly right. A real person says, "Gimme a burger ana cuppa coffee." There was a little more to it than just that, but you get the idea.

So then you ask yourself, *"What am I selling? What am I trying to get the other person to do?"* You know, the old *Who? What? When? Where?* and *Why?*

What is the emotion at that moment? Is it sad, happy, sexy, angry, sarcastic, or shy? Or what emotion am I trying to evoke? Is it excitement, yearning, or something else? Is the product new? Or is it on sale? Why is it different from any other similar product? And remember, *you must really love* the product, whatever it is.

Then: What voice should I use. Am I talking one to one with a friend? Or am I addressing a small or large group. Is my character tough or mean, or is he an old softy? Am I a human, or an inanimate object? I once auditioned for the voice of a hot dog and the director said, "Oh, you are so close. But you're doing a hamburger not a hot dog." (He was the hot dog.) Sometimes you are told that the client asked for "friendly-authority." Well, you can't be both. So you must make a decision. Do you have an authoritative sound, in which case all you have to do is be friendly? Or are you the friendly sounding type who should now ramp up the authoritativeness in your delivery?

And, by the way … don't regard the audition as "the audition." Think of it as "the job." You have to be on your total game *now!* Not later when you get the gig—or you just might not get the gig.

Some actors will pick up a script and while they're looking through it they think to themselves, "Bullshit … bullshit … my part … bullshit … bullshit … my part …" I must admit to having done that myself at times. What a bad habit that is. In order to know what the hell you're reading, you have to read it *all*. That means the direction, the other people's parts—everything. I guarantee you that if you make a habit of not reading the whole script, it will come back to bite you in the butt one day.

# ADDITIONAL TIPS FOR SUCCESS

*Voice-over classes.* In the "Voice-Over Resource Guide," published quarterly by Dave and Dave Publications (and now available on the web), there are over ninety entries of people who teach voice-over classes of one sort or another. Some of them are conducted by friends of mine. Some are by people I've never met. Some are held by casting directors, and some by producers and studio technicians. Some teach animation, while others teach dialects, promos—even trailers. Some teach kids. Some teach privately, and some teach in studio settings, while others use their homes. The cost of classes ranges anywhere from $30 an evening to $200 an hour. Classes are conducted nightly, daily, and on weekends, or you can arrange a schedule to suit your own needs. There are classes for beginners, intermediates, and advanced. A few teachers will let you audit one of their classes.

*Demos.* Some of the teachers also make demo recordings. The fees for demos run anywhere from $50 to $1,500. I can't stress enough the value of a good demo reel. First, it literally creates you to those who don't know you exist. Second, it demonstrates your talent. Third, it shows your credits. Since part of it is the creation process, I've always argued that your picture should be on its cover somewhere.

When I was in radio, I was called upon to do a lot of personal appearances. Whenever I met my listeners in person for the first time, I was almost always "wrong." They had conjured up a vision in their heads of what I should look like, and I never matched the vision.

"You can't be Jack Angel; he's a great big guy with broad shoulders and a narrow waist." I swear to God, a female listener actually said that to me once.

If you have your picture somewhere on the CD box, when people listen to the reel, they'll be looking at your face and attaching your face to your sound. Then, when they meet you, you'll be "right." Some people have argued against that position, but I think the benefits far outweigh any problems that may arise about how you look.

My tapes have always been compilations of commercials and animated characters that I did over a period of time. And the tape sounds like it. There are different energies on different projects and different energy quotients from studio to studio and mic to mic When you have a demo reel dummied up in a studio, all the spots are usually recorded on the same day, with the same energy and the same room ambience. It's a dead giveaway that you dummied it up. Not that that won't work to some degree. I just think it's better if it sounds like a whole lot of tracks recorded at different times—as if you already have a career cooking.

Another thing you should look out for is recording a "famous" commercial as if it is yours. Don't do Visa spots. Ed Grover used to be the voice of Visa for a hundred years. The same thing goes with Lexus commercials. Jim Sloyan was the only announcer Lexus had ever had until just recently. And for an even longer time than that, Mason Adams, until his death a few years ago, was the only person to say, "With a name like Smucker's, it *has* to be good." (Gary Owens did say once—with his hand cupping his ear—"With a name like Smucker's, it *had better* be good.")

You want to create the strongest context possible. Doing famous spots on your demo reel just takes away from your credibility.

The way things work today, you can take copies of your spots, real or not, feed them into your computer, and edit them the way you want. Sound Forge is a good, easy-to-use editing program that will do quite nicely in a PC. In the long run, it'll be a better reel and cost you less, and you maintain control.

Throughout my career, every time I'd do a new project, I'd want it on my demo reel. I recently threw away an apple box filled with dub-masters I had made and then changed because I got another job I liked and wanted to add to the rest.

You don't want to be paying someone to add things to your reel every time you get something new. I bought a four-deck CD burner so I can grind them out faster. If you plan to do a lot of CDs or DVDs, this might be the way to go. I'll sell you mine.

You can also make your own CDs and CD labels. I use CD Stomper in my computer, so I can print my own labels and jewel case inserts. All this gives me total flexibility to change anything, anytime I choose.

If you do decide to have a professional make your tape or CD for you, be aware that he or she probably doesn't know you as well as you do and may leave out the very essence of who you are. I've listened to many tapes where the strongest attributes of the talent were absent because the actor let the pro run the session, without giving any personal input.

At one point I decided to be completely innovative, so I created *video* demos—one for commercials, one for animation, and one for trailers and promos. I collected a lot of spots and animated episodes. Those that I couldn't get from producers, I recorded off the air by putting a tape in the VCR and leaving it on all day. The problem with that idea was that the video was so strong that once the demo started to play, the person watching it got engrossed in the video production of each item, and the voice got lost in the process.

I asked a good friend to listen and critique one of my video tapes.

When it was over, I asked, "Well?"

He responded, "Damn! I'm sorry. I got so wrapped up in watching the 'vids,' I forgot to listen."

Making video demos to promote voice-overs is very expensive and, quite frankly, not worth the cost. I did, however, create a mailer I sent out to remind those who got the tape to watch it.

The top ten talent agencies have anywhere from 65 to 150 commercial actors in just the men's category. There are almost as many women, along with lots of animation performers, plus announcers who just do promos and trailers. There are a couple of thousand men and a couple of thousand women in Los Angeles alone, all looking for work as voice-over artists. And those are just the ones with demo reels. There are a whole bunch of celebrities and on-camera actors who also, from time to time, do voice-overs. This talent pool is filled with some of the most amazing people you have ever heard. They are the best in the world. You can let that intimidate you, or you can consider it a challenge and work hard to become one of them.

*Phoning it in.* Now, with the advent of digital delivery systems such as ISDN lines and MP3 e-mails, anyone, anywhere, can get into the game, which further dilutes the possibilities of you getting work.

If you're going to do promos, you almost *have* to have access to an ISDN line, since many TV stations would rather deal with announcers who stay home and merely "phone it in." That gives producers much more flexibility as to hours and studio availability.

For years, John Driscoll has been doing it that way with promos and news headlines for TV and radio stations all over the country. It's a cottage industry with John. When he moved to Marin County, north of San Francisco, he realized that there are frequent power outages, so he hooked up a generator that kicks on when the power kicks off. He also has dual computers, dual fax machines, and dual ISDN systems, so that no matter what happens he's on the air, ready to go.

Some of this may begin to sound daunting. I don't tell you all of this to discourage you from entering the game, but to warn you to be ready when you do jump in.

*Staying healthy.* Part of being ready is being healthy. Colds are the bane of the voice actor. Although there is a time just before you're over the cold when your voice really sounds deep and throaty, it's better to never have a cold.

Easier said than done, you say? Not so! John Cygan and I share the same family physician, Dr. Rob Huizenga in Beverly Hills. Maybe you've seen him on TV as the medical authority on *The Biggest Loser*. John asked him one day how he stayed healthy since he is constantly surrounded by sick people all day every day. Rob replied that he never touches himself above the chest unless he washes his hands first. Cold germs are introduced into your body through your nose and eyes by you sticking your fingers there after you've come in contact with someone having a cold. The germs get into the mucus or tears. Arlene and I carry around one of those antibacterial lotions and every time we shake hands with someone or touch an escalator, hand rail, menu, or any number of other bacteria-laden objects, we rub a little lotion on our hands. It's amazing how well it works.

# AFTRA AND SAG

If you want to be a major player, you will be required to belong to both Screen Actors Guild and the American Federation of Television and Radio Artists, our two unions. At the time of this writing there is a strong possibility the two unions will merge into one.

You are not required to work at either union office. Working for a union in any capacity *will not further your acting career*. Working for the union, or serving on the board of directors, will suck up your energy and time ... time that should be devoted to developing your self and your career. Go to a couple of meetings and watch what happens. If that sort of thing appeals to you, just understand what you are getting into.

I spent a solid year on the SAG Animation Negotiating Committee, and it was probably the most frustrating year of my life. The meetings were mostly at night, and I came home every evening around midnight with smoke pouring out of my ears. My wife, who was certain I was going to have a stroke, made me promise that once the negotiations were settled, I'd never get involved like that with a union again.

During a disastrous six-month commercial strike in 2000, I did attend lots of meetings and even offered my own personal input from time to time, but I will never again participate as a committee member. It has to do with your purpose in life. If you want to further your career, do that. If you want to further the success of the union, do that.

Arlene Thornton's Studio City office is in the same building where the AFTRA/SAG Federal Credit Union used to be, and whenever there was an upcoming vote on anything, I'd see unionists standing outside of the credit union passing out flyers. Sometimes they were there all day. I know a couple of actors who couldn't take the elevator up to the fourth floor to audition because they had committed their time to trying to get an election swayed one way or another.

When you start missing appointments because of union activity, your career is in jeopardy. Your unions will survive quite nicely without your continued involvement. Your career will not.

# I Have More Than Myself to Thank

Since there are no negatives, I would like to thank all those people who fired me right out of radio. Were it not for you, I might still be saying "this is" and "that was," and doing time and temperature. I'd also like to acknowledge all those people who hired me over the years and kept me from selling shoes. And thanks to all the people who didn't hire me, thus leaving space for those who did. In my world everybody gets a "thank you."

There are some individuals whom I credit with having given my voice-over career the nurturing it needed to flourish.

First were Gary Owens and Bob Colvin.

Shortly after I arrived at KMPC in Los Angeles, I made my first commercial demo reel and played it for Gary. He unselfishly introduced me to his voice agent, Bob Colvin of Abrams–Rubaloff, who agreed to represent me. That kicked everything off. (Shortly after I joined Bob at A-R, he left and opened his own agency, Carey, Phelps & Colvin.)

Second is Bob Lloyd, the original "Voicecaster."

Abrams Rubaloff and Associates was one of the bigger commercial agencies at the time - but I found myself on what might be called "the B team."

Richard Lawrence, Colvin's replacement was the agent in charge of voice-overs then, and one day he said to me just out of the blue, "I wish I could do more for you, but my hands are tied."

"What do you mean?" I asked.

"Well, we represent guys who make a quarter of a million dollars a year doing this [a lot of money in those days], and we have to keep them happy no matter what. So, like, if an agency asks for only five people on the audition, and one of these heavy-weights starts complaining that he hasn't been out enough lately, we might bump you and replace you with him."

"It sounds as if you have me on the second team, Richard." I said.

"Yeah," he acknowledged. "It's kinda like that."

"I've never been on anyone's second string, Richard, and I'm sure as hell not going to be on yours," I snapped back.

It was about that time that Bob Lloyd joined Ann Wright as the voice agent. He sent word to me through a mutual friend that if I was unhappy where I was, I should come and talk to him. Bob went on to tell me he was starting from scratch, so there wasn't much of a department yet, but he assured me that I would be his "all everything" if I joined him. And true to his word, I was.

Was it better to be on a big agency's second string, or on a small, hungry agency's first string? The answer for me was obvious.

Bob and I actually had a race to see who could generate more income for me—him or me.

Next comes Alan Barzman.

One day I stopped by Alan Barzman's office and introduced myself. Barz had worked at KEX, in Portland, a few years before me, so we had that in our history. After about an hour into our conversation, he asked me, "What can I do for you?"

I responded, "Well, an Alan Barzman radio spot would sure give my demo reel a lot of credibility. You are, after all, the reigning master of the radio spot."

"Oh! No problem!" he said.

Barz began hiring me regularly on his productions. This went on for a couple of years, just when I needed it most. He did warn me once by saying, "I fall out of love with people, and when that happens, I'll let you know."

One of the best things Barz did for me is he gave me "human lessons." Remember I told you I couldn't *hear* that I sounded like a radio announcer even when I ordered a hamburger and a coffee at Bob's Big Boy. Barz made me read out of the newspaper until I began to sound like the guy next door. That opened a whole other avenue of work for me.

And one day, he said, "I think you hang around here too much."

And I knew the love affair was over. But not before he had helped to create me as a top guy in the business.

The fourth was the late Bill Bell.

Bill Bell was the owner of Bell Sound Studios in Hollywood. Barz did most of his recording at Bell Sound. Bill and I became solid friends, and since Bill and I had been fired from radio by the same guy, we also had common ground there.

So whenever Bill did any casting, he always threw a few spots my way. Once, when I was sitting in his lobby, schmoozing with a couple of voice people, he poked his head out of the studio and asked if I had few minutes to spare. He had just finished some "Reagan for Governor" commercials for Ronald Reagan's first run for public office, and I became the announcer on the legal tags: "The preceding paid for by the Reagan for Governor Committee."

Bill also hired me on some national Chevy commercials and other campaigns that contributed to the bank account as well.

It was good luck to visit Bill a couple of times a week, as long as I didn't wear out my welcome.

I had always been able to do funny voices and impressions, ever since I was a kid. But it was Wally Burr who hired me at Hanna/Barbera to work on *Superfriends* and other H/B productions. He continued to hire me when he did the casting for and directed almost all the Marvel shows, like *G.I. Joe* and *The Transformers*. That got me started in animation and helped create the credibility I needed to continue.

Another contributor to my voice-over career was Jeremiah Comey, who teaches acting in Hollywood.

When I told you that Alan Barzman gave me human lessons, it was true. But, I cheated a little. As I said earlier, it was easier for me to actually create a character that was my "real person" voice than it was to totally rid my self of sounding like an announcer all the time.

I enrolled in Jeremiah Comey's classes and that's when I finally got it about being able to drop my announcer self when it was appropriate. This was a cold-reading-exercise class in which you couldn't run your "act." You had to try to read your partner and respond off of him or her. And even though this class was geared to film acting, it became invaluable when I used the techniques I learned there to enhance my range in voicing commercials. I highly recommend Jeremiah's classes to all actors.

I can't forget John Luma, who hired me at NBC, and Paula Cwikly, who kept me there.

And I would be remiss if I didn't mention Mickie McGowan, the head of a looping group that does a lot of work for Disney, Pixar, and Fox. Without her, I probably would never have been in any of their shows.

And I must thank one more person, my wife, Arlene. Some know her as Arlene Angel and some know her as Arlene Thornton. But however you know her, she's the best thing that ever happened to me. I give her 100 percent of me and she returns the favor by adding it to everything she has and giving it back.

# RÉSUMÉS

Keep your résumé up-to-date. If you keep the information on your computer, you can add to it whenever you do anything new. Here is mine.

## PROMOS & TRAILERS

NBC Promos
WB Promos
ABC Promos
CBS Promos
Cox Broadcasting
TBS Tabloid
*Master and Commander* Trailers
*Extra* Promos
E! Channel Promos
*Bram Stoker's Dracula* Trailers
McDonald's / *Jurassic Park* Promo
*The Tonight Show Starring Johnny Carson* Promos

## COMMERCIALS

[Over the years, I've done so many commercials, it would be impossible to list them all. These are a few of the more memorable ones.]

Voice of "Smokey the Bear"
T-Mobile
MSN Direct
POM Wonderful Pomegranate Juice
Amdro Herbicides
City of Hope Cancer Centers
White Castle
Goodyear
Verizon
NIKE
Macys.com
Sugar Bowl Ski Resort
U.S. Forest Service
Nationwide Insurance
Mattel's "Mad Scientist"
Mattel's "Judge Dredd" Action Figure
Tabasco Steak Sauce
Amoco Gasoline
Honda Motorcycles
Sunkist Oranges
AM/PM Mini-Marts/ARCO
K-Swiss
United Health Plan
The Medicine Shoppe Pharmacies

## ON-CAMERA COMMERCIALS

| | |
|---|---|
| Kodak | Scrooge |
| Burger Chef | Scrooge |
| Bank of Arizona | Scrooge |
| Universal Studios | Dracula |
| KFC | Abraham Lincoln |
| Carl's Jr. /Magic Mountain | Wizard |

## TELEVISION SHOWS

| | |
|---|---|
| *The Young & the Restless* | Judge Kline (On-Camera) |
| *Passions* | |
| *Scarecrow and Mrs. King* | |
| *Step by Step* | TV Announcer |
| *The John Larroquette Show* | TV Spot Announcer |
| *Crime Story* | Show Narrator |
| *Harry and the Hendersons* | TV Wrestler |
| *Babes* | Baseball Play-by-Play Announcer |
| *Growing Pains* | TV Evangelist |
| *Silver Spoons* | Chess Player |
| *The Six Million Dollar Man* | Tower Operator |

## FEATURE FILMS—VOICE

| | |
|---|---|
| Steven Spielberg's *A.I.* | Voice of Teddy |
| *Vendetta* | Old Gaspare |
| *The Fifth Element* | Alien Commander |
| *Deterrence* | Secretary of Defense |
| *Beetlejuice* | Gourd-Head Preacher |
| *Trenchcoat* | Head Kidnapper |
| *Funny Lady* | Radio Announcer |
| *The World's Greatest Lover* | Voice on the Record |
| *Hook* | Pirates |

| | |
|---|---|
| *Deal of the Century* | Commercial Announcer |
| *Mom and Dad Save the World* | Creature |
| *I Am My Résumé* | Stan Angeles |
| Mole-Richardson | Industrial Narrator |
| USC Football | Industrial Narrator |

## INTERACTIVE CD'S—VOICE

| | |
|---|---|
| *RESIDENT EVIL,* | |
| *OPERATION RACOON CITY* | Just Cause Productions |
| *GOTHIC III* | Activision |
| *SAINTS ROW* | Savant |
| *TITAN'S QUEST* | Savant |
| *SHADOW OF ROME* | Capcom |
| *EVERQUEST* | On-Line Game |
| *DREAMFALL* | Aspyr |
| *SHADOW OF ROME* | Pax Romano |
| *Dark Forces* | Lucas Arts |
| *Full Throttle* | Lucas Arts |
| *Grim Fandango* | Lucas Arts |
| *Outlaws* | Lucas Arts |
| *The Dark Eye* | Inscape |
| *Magic of Shannara* | Advance Concepts |

## ANIMATED FILMS—VOICE

| | |
|---|---|
| *Dr. Seuss' The Lorax* | Universal |
| *Monster University.* | Disney/Pixar |
| *Smurfs Dance Party* | Sony |
| *Toy Story III* | Disney/Pixar |
| *Horton Hears a Who* | FOX |
| *Ice Age II* | FOX |
| *Cars* | Pixar/Disney |
| *Finding Nemo* | Pixar/Disney |

| | |
|---|---|
| *Monsters, Inc.* | Pixar/Disney |
| *Toy Story* | Pixar/Disney |
| *Toy Story II* | Pixar/Disney |
| *A Bug's Life* | Pixar/Disney |
| *Spirited Away* | Disney |
| *Ratchet and Clank* | Disney |
| *Treasure Planet* | Disney |
| *Atlantis* | Disney |
| *Tarzan* | Disney |
| *Land of Enchantment* | Disney |
| *Lilo and Stitch* | Disney |
| *The Hunchback of Notre Dame* | Disney |
| *Aladdin* | Disney |
| *Beauty and the Beast* | Disney |
| *Little Mermaid* | Disney |
| *Who Framed Roger Rabbit* | Disney |
| 2 *Roger Rabbit* Shorts | Disney |
| *Porco Rosso* | Disney |
| *The Iron Giant* | Warner Bros. |
| *Quest for Camelot* | Warner Bros. |
| *The Prince of Egypt* | DreamWorks SKG |
| *Amazing Stories* ("Family Dog") | Amblin Entertainment |
| *Balto* | Amblin Entertainment |
| *The Arabian Knight* | Miramax |
| *G.I. Joe: The Movie* | Marvel |
| *Blondie and Dagwood* | Marvel |
| *Transformers: The ,Movie 1986* | Marvel |
| *The Legend of Paul Bunyan* | Bosustow |

## ANIMATED SERIES—VOICE

(Regular or Recurring Roles)

| | |
|---|---|
| *El Tigre* | Nickelodeon |
| *Darkwing Duck* | Disney (Liquidator) |
| *Tail Spin* | Disney (Commissar) |
| *Spiderman* | Marvel (Nick Fury) |
| *G.I. Joe* | Marvel (Wet Suit) |
| *Jem!* | Marvel (Jem's Father) |
| *Transformers* | Marvel (Ramjet, AstroTrain, others) |
| *Peter Pan and The Pirates* | Fox (Mullins and Cookson) |
| *SuperFriends* | H-B (Hawkman and Flash) |
| *Pole Position* | DiC Enterprises (Dr. Zachary) |
| *Voltron* | WorldEvents(Hazar,Zarkon, others) |

## ANIMATION—VOICE

(Guest Performer)

| | |
|---|---|
| *Casper* | Universal |
| *Mask* | Film Roman |
| *Sinbad* | Fred Wolf |
| *Ninja Turtles* | Fred Wolf |
| *Bonkers* | Disney |
| *Duck Tales* | Disney |
| *Duck Daze* | Disney |
| *Back to the Future* | Amblin Entertainment |
| *Captain Planet* | Hanna/Barbera |
| *Cowboys from Moo Mesa* | Hanna/Barbera |
| *Smurfs* | Hanna/Barbera |
| *Scooby-Doo* | Hanna/Barbera |
| *Space Cats* | Marvel |
| *Prince Valiant* | Valiant |

| | |
|---|---|
| *Dennis the Menace* | DiC Enterprises |
| *ProStars* | DiC Enterprises |
| *Ring Raiders* | DiC Enterprises |
| *Denver, the Last Dinosaur* | |

## RADIO

(Disc Jockey)

| | |
|---|---|
| KYOS | Merced, California |
| KJAX | Santa Rosa, California |
| KJBS | San Francisco, California |
| KOLO | Reno, Nevada |
| KOWL | Lake Tahoe, Nevada (Simulcast with KOLO) |
| KOLO TV | Reno, Nevada (Weatherman and Host) |
| KEX | Portland, Oregon |
| KMPC | Los Angeles, California |
| KFI | Los Angeles, California |
| KIIS AM | Los Angeles, California |
| KFI | Los Angeles, California |

## THEATER

| | |
|---|---|
| Contra Costa JC | *The Magnanimous Lover* |
| San Francisco State | *Caesar and Cleopatra* |
| | *On the Town* |
| Portland Civic Theatre | *Finian's Rainbow* |
| | *A Thousand Clowns* |
| | *Will Success Spoil Rock Hunter* |

# OTHER BOOKS TO READ

*Word of Mouth* by Susan Blu and Molly Ann Mullin.

This is the most complete book I've seen on how to do voice-overs. Susan has worked as an actress, nightclub singer, voice-over artist—she was the Pillsbury Dough Girl—and for a long time ran her own studio in Sherman Oaks. She's very savvy about the business and together with Molly has written a great book.

| | |
|---|---|
| *Hearing Voices* | by Alan Barzman |
| *Greatest Cartoon Voice Tricks* | by Pat Fraley |
| *Scenes for Actors and Voices* | by Daws Butler |
| *My Life as a Ten-Year-Old Boy* | by Nancy Cartwright— |
| | The Voice of Bart Simpson |

# THAT'S A RAP!

A lot of times in this book, I've discussed context—whether you hold things as positive or negative, et cetera. You can say all this stuff is just a pile of crap and forget it. That's okay. If you decide that, then none of this will work for you. But understand something: a few of your competitors are going to validate some or all of it. And there's the rub. He or she will be out there putting a lot of this into play—while you are not—and they'll be creating big geodesic balls.

My attitude has always been *"Go for it!"* Run with the hounds nipping at your heels. Live dangerously. Don't play it safe; take a chance. Your aliveness will be in betting on yourself. Invest in *you*.